I0089233

A Highland Holiday

A Vacation in Verse

STOCKWELL
PUBLISHERS SINCE 1898

J. B. Dundee

Published in 2022 by
J. B. Dundee
in association with
Arthur H Stockwell Ltd
West Wing Studios
Unit 166, The Mall
Luton, Bedfordshire
ahstockwell.co.uk

Copyright © 2022 J. B. Dundee

The right of J. B. Dundee to be identified as the author
of this work has been asserted in accordance with
the Copyright, Designs and Patents Act 1988.

All rights reserved. No reproduction, copy or transmission
of this publication may be made without express prior
written permission. No paragraph of this publication may be
reproduced, copied or transmitted except with express prior
written permission or in accordance with the provisions of the
Copyright Act 1956 (as amended). Any person who commits
any unauthorised act in relation to this publication may be
liable to criminal prosecution and civil claims for damage.

British Library Cataloguing-in-Publication Data: A catalogue
record for this book is available from the British Library.
ISBN 9780722351673

The views and opinions expressed within this
book belong to the author and do not necessarily
reflect those of the Arthur H Stockwell Ltd.

To my darling wife, Gillian

By the same author:

A Collection of Verse, Volume I
A Collection of Verse, Volume II
A Collection of Verse, Volume III
A Collection of Verse, Volume IV

Only once across the Border does for me the holiday start.
Farewell as I leave England, now onward I shall follow my heart.
Whilst in the mirror she falls away, through the Lowlands I proceed.
Past Gretna's lovers' lure and signs for Ecclefechan … hard to read.
Then on to, into and through the shires of Lanark, Stirling and Perth,
with mounting excitement to be at my most prized place 'pon this earth.

To our usual stop-off at the Harrods of the North first
and thus into a world of the well-off or flush tourist immersed.
Gasp at the cost of items cashmere … yet 'tis 'mere cash' after all
and holiday we are on. … I shall just gawp and o'er them enthral.
'Pon all ways to look, tweed, tartan and troves of material wealth.
Oh, what joy could be had if my bank accounts were in hearty health!

The House of Bruar.

Should the notion your fancy tickle, for a while more to tarry,
fasten your boots, follow the routes uphill from the River Garry.
As down they gush, by the dramatic falls steadily you shall climb
and feeble feel at the torrents' side … view your life so brief in time.
Purely from water's labours, rock formations, sculptures twist and squeeze,
as, for the nation's bard, the surrounding land be awash with trees.

1

Views of the Falls of Bruar (best seen after torrential rain).

From the House of Bruar northward, through increasingly craggy land,
winding by the highest distillery in this realm white and grand,
by snow gates and markers staggered and all around the sights excite,
with the growing contentment that my bones shall rest well from this night.
Briskly, downhill from Dalwhinnie 'long Wade's old military road,
where back in Scotland's grim, turbulent past oppressive redcoats strode.

2

Dalwhinnie Distillery, with clouds behind covering the hilltop.

Down right at the phone box 'pon a one-car track we take at the bend.
Eyes fast bleary, 'tis good to know we have reached our journey's end.
Whilst for oncomers watching, some more yards further we pass the farm,
then over the burn another right turn to this place full of charm.
Gravel neath crunches as we come to our destination's halt
and all which encircles I can but look at and as one exalt.

From the car to step and a feeling of fond reunion is felt,
with the belief that I have now had more favourable cards dealt.
No lands, real or fabled, better these. … Thanks to be here I utter.
Narnia, or the land of Oz … I could be no more aflutter.
Thus through the door – left unlocked, of course, for not in the suburbs now,
with the only onlooker likely to be a crow, sheep or cow.

Once more I am arrived with 'yond my Monadhliath mountain range.
'Tis such a great comfort to know it shall ne'er but for seasons change.
By Laggan, on to spread one side of the valley from west to east.
To look 'pon its vista is my most thrillful inner child released.
Tears quite easily he could shed, for he has missed them till now so.
As they begin, how I pray the coming weeks more than most might slow.

Monadhliath Mountains.

And oh, what glory senses flood, to be where you feel you belong!
For the slightest aspect is all it takes to bring my soul to song.
With each blink of the eyes, photo-like captured and forever held,
whilst for this duration are all disquiets and dark thoughts dispelled.
Alike with planets, the near-perfect harmony aligned within
brings a lightness of spirit seldom attained which flowers therein.

What of our dwelling? Has it altered since last we resided?
Are there the same comforts and such as previously provided?
So a quick foray round and all seems sound to me up and downstairs.
Most important for us, post trudge … two blue cloth-clad recliner chairs.
When tendons are tender, joints are jiggered and fatigue lead-like weighs,
pray ne'er underestimate the vital part their comfiness plays.

In the lounge, central of the long outer wall stands the open fire,
with stone surround, ready for lighting when I for the day retire.
Many an hour I hope to spend bathed in its flickering glow;
meanwhile, there are cupboards to fill and luggage 'pon the bed to throw.
Quietly ignored by our grazing neighbour with tatty fleece,
we unpack and call home, for now, this cottage 'pon the hill of peace.

Holiday cottage – Creag-na-Sanais.

For our first walk at last poised and to commence I cannot wait.
So to the McPherson cairn we make, found through the black iron gate,
near the 'Centre of Scotland', as declares a plaque 'cross yonder way.
A spot … spellbound to stand, 'fore the wide flat valley with snaking Spey,
which looks to hold time and stretch on to forever. … 'Tis just stunning,
as I watch the sky reflect back from the distant river running.

Cairn and view to the west.

To the east.

For indeed, the same as that for my whole world is Scotland's centre
and am forever pulled once I within its gravity enter.
All which may be seen from here and for miles in any direction,
will stir my blood and from my psyche rouse a primal connection.
'Pon nowhere else but Highland soil do I feel as part of the land.
'Tis a feeling I have long had, though even I scarce understand.

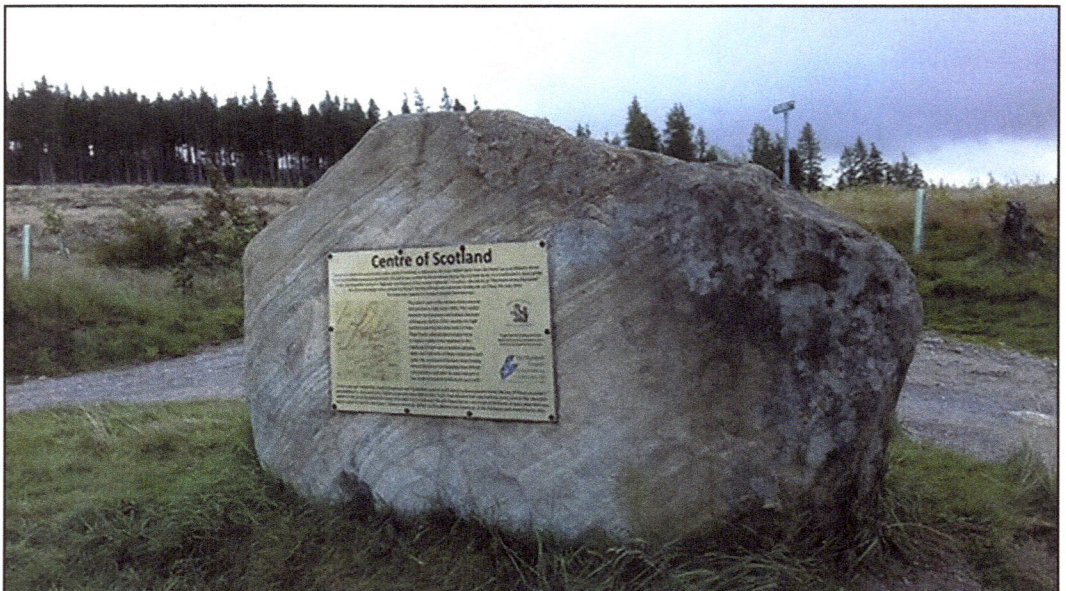

The Centre of Scotland.

6

'Pon the return, with scant warning … though of little surprise to me,
as if to reaffirm where we are – for no telltale signs to see—
arises from the calm a deft, wetting meld as windward walking
and in but seconds the surging gusts have each forward step balking.
Yet once down the brae, as 'twixt the depth of birch and pine I go on,
that which thus leaves me soggy-limbed so swift as whence it came is gone.

Part of the long walk home, now showing no sign of the wind and rain which wet me.

The stream flowing down to the bridge then River Spey shows how rocky the terrain is.

Cows watch us passing. Beyond the woodland, heather gives way to rocky crags.

Along past the still on-looking cattle, in the rough pasture field—
little use for to try and plough; only rocky rubble would yield.
Even they the near silence respect and stand or sit quite muted.
Not the long-haired Highland brutes, which
around here would look more suited.
Whilst chewing, they stare at these two walking oddities going by,
perhaps more used to the swish of cars as they to the campsite fly.

Back to base, with a stack of kindling and logs waiting to be lit
and those aforementioned cosy chairs such a pleasure 'pon to sit.
So shoes are off then slippers on to rest my chafed and well-walked feet,
to bide till later to have the tipple which makes my day complete.
We dine, then upon the comfy seats recline, well fed and tired;
yet not once might I think to complain of aches and pains acquired.

Is nigh each room a gallery akin, as views 'yond window frames
show picturesque scenes of slopes and peaks,
though unknown by most their names.
I should merrily survey them all, till the night leaves naught to spy.
Who needs television's bland distractions when such 'pon doorsteps lie?
Once descends the darkness, mirrors become the glass's only use.
So fireside I settle, till its flames lethargy shall induce.

A scenic view from every window.

A pleasant day indeed was had, and I hope a precedent set—
the first of many which I pray will be with the same relish met.
Though the rain has lashed and through to my
cold skin by the wind was blown,
I was kept cheered by the scenery 'pon every corner shown.
Time now this evening to round off with a glass of liquid heaven.
Though soon leaves me drowsy, my demeanour it shall always leaven.

To temper first with dash of water, where'pon such flavours to free.
'Tis to capture its essence and have the Highlands lie within me.
A taste worth the acquiring, for a further dimension to lend,
as from the crystal sipped, all the notes thus upon my palate blend,
allowing another sense to rejoice in what this land offers.
Once to pass my lips, I shall ne'er begrudge the outlay of coffers.

If you are a whisky admirer, then whilst you be up this way
you may wish to tour a distillery … perhaps one by the Spey.
Part of the visit experience is to try a tot or two;
if on one you have ne'er been, it might be of interest to do.
In truth, I must confess, over the years I have been on many.
To me, 'twas more like a pilgrimage … but did not cost a penny.

Alas 'twould seem like everywhere else levies have been introduced
and once again the poor tourist is being financially juiced.
Though if you can afford it, for a one-off treat then go ahead,
but I would rather they might rethink then cease their charging instead.
I should vent my displeasure by no more buying their single malt….
But let us be sensible – 'tis not the whisky which is at fault.

A wee early evening dram … or two.

Soon, the first bedtime. … What a challenge for us townies it can be,
as off with the bulb in a click goes the ability to see!
For 'tis slightly unnerving when nightfall leaves me with sightless eyes,
swift within such pitch-black plunged, whilst
to pick out shapes my vision tries.
Lest the moon as a nightlight serves, as it has 'pon visits afore,
for a short while we may leave a lamp lit beyond the bedroom door.

As it begins … 'pon the skylight glass above my drowsing repose,
I listen to the rain gently gain then fade as I deeper doze.
Though a glow may show on high, the clouds appear too tightly amassed.
'Twould seem my chance to see the moon before I fall asleep has passed.
Yet in the early hours I awake and look around the room,
as a shawl of purest milky beams has driven away the gloom.

When lights first go off it's hard to tell if eyes are open or closed. Let's hope for moonlight.

I lift my head and gaze aloft beyond the wooden window frame;
and though eyes blurry, the sight they see my sense of wonder shall claim.
In patches of clear black sky the moon sits proud, rounded and gleaming
and once broken through the thinning veil its lovely light is streaming.
Glaring so, it all but one blots out the great assembly of stars.
Now to sleep I return and leave it with the company of Mars.

Thus the morning arrives, with the farm dogs eager to start their day.
However, I, less enthused, may choose a little longer to stay.
Neath the covers I shall listen for the things which cannot be heard:
a motorway encroaching 'pon the breeze, ne'er once by me preferred;
or aircraft o'erhead passing as the road outside thrums with cars.
Not here, for nothing 'yond my lazy lie this blissful moment jars.

Round eight o'clock the herd is heard as the farmer leads them along;
across the broad valley plain, behind his quad bike follows the throng,
whilst bulls first their lungs fill then with loud bassy bellows fill the air.
The noise permeates the still and lets us all know that they are there.
Breakfast beckons, so with a yawn and a sigh I shall rise and shine
and say fare thee well for now, my noisy distant neighbours bovine.

11

Far across the valley the cattle's cries rang out.

Soon, off out to the Co-op at Newtonmore village for shopping.
For me to first see this store, I could not stop my jaw from dropping,
as 'twas once the grand locale of the wonderful Waltzing Waters,
which brought much joy to so many, including my two dear daughters.
With a cinema-like interior, though with curtains … no screen,
instead was an enjoyable performance I had ne'er fore seen.

A profusion of splashing fountains shone with brightly coloured lights,
with pleasing varied music interwoven to go with the sights,
in sprays and jets which fanned and flared to keep the audience enthralled.
To come back and find it all demolished, I really was appalled.
That it should exist no longer I truly think is such a shame,
and it only goes to show … not all things up here remain the same.

Though change be the cradle of nostalgia, I welcome it here less
than anywhere else I chance to see its slow yet certain progress.
For things these parts found which add their appeal, I have a simple view:
they should remain in the present, to enjoy now then next time too.
Once gone they are forever thus and their like will ne'er be again.
Lost to the past – just something people remember from way back when.

Newtonmore Co-op, once the sight of the Waltzing Waters.

Preferring quiet, the bustle of Aviemore comes as a shock,
as in their droves traffic and tourists here from the north and south flock.
Hikers and bikers, all shapes and sizes, from all parts of the world,
'pon four sides round me surge as I feel into chaos promptly hurled.
Of course the wife just drifts through shops like a butterfly on the breeze.
She cares not of crowds, hence no swelling volume shall cause her unease.

On soon my stomach alerts me that lunchtime has almost arrived;
so now to leave these streets, 'pon which I feel I have barely survived.
A treat is in order – if it comes at some expense, what the hell!
Thus we smarten ourselves up and move on to the Cairngorm Hotel.
To take lunch in three-star tartan plushness was really quite the thrill,
although I must confess my wallet winced when I received the bill.

But the food was good, the ambience nice and the staff were pleasant.
A rare extravagance 'twas for me, a penny-pinching peasant.
Then to the station o'er the road and the footbridge you should traverse,
for 'pon Platform Three you will see the modern world for now disperse.
The Strathspey Railway to a simpler time, long gone, will take you back,
to be by a steam engine hauled on a scenic ten miles of track.

The Cairngorm Hotel.

'Tis intriguing how a railway does not the countryside despoil.
Steam trains enhance the backdrop, despite the puffing smoke, soot and oil.
They look to be as alive and entitled to be there in flight
as horses, sheep and deer, who scatter from them in panic and fright.
They may also in a small way my faith in humanity save.
Who can resist, when steam trains go by, at complete strangers to wave?

The Strathspey Railway, with the Cairngorm mountain range in the background.

Some distance 'yond stores and streets the Cairn
Gorm rises with cloud-cloaked peak.
When last here 'twas a trice to surmount this beast, beautifully bleak,
'pon its presently defunct funicular – quite a ride to take
to the top station o'er 3,000 feet! Such views … if clouds would break.
Now just the base station it must be … though not nearly as much fun,
so I weave and wind where reindeer roam and hope for clear sky and sun.

Cairngorm base station for mountain railway.

I remember well that last venture toward the summit by rail;
for once 'pon the balcony arrived I found myself flailed by hail.
By a thick fog beset, the view was no more than ten yards ahead,
and I wondered if I should have stayed down in Aviemore instead.
Then in wisps and swirls, like a dream scene clouds briefly apart drifted
and I like Zeus peered down to the valley for that short while gifted.

'Tis funny how moments like such can be so fleeting in their time,
yet within the mind they engrave themselves so deeply and sublime.
For but one minute either side and the glimpse may ne'er have been had,
and hence missed would have been an abiding mental keepsake to add.
Oft 'tis brief sights which so enrich and induce an awestruck intake;
and when from the memory drawn, a marvellous montage they make.

Looking back down the road from the base station.

With swish of nylon leggings to my late afternoon walk I take,
and from a sodden gusting 'pon my back a decent pace I make.
Alone if needs I like to go a mile or so up to the bridge.
'Tis a mild exertion 'long the lane 'pon the valley's southern ridge.
For me, this little effort gives a large reward in its displays,
as there and back along the track is a sight to see 'pon both ways.

The bridge on the valley track, looking back towards the cottage.

'Twould suggest the roughest weather is blown along o'er from the west;
though moving east is its load released, to lighten up … less oppressed.
For to gaze one way is all haze and greys – angry-looking indeed.
The other view is skies of blue with thin clouds too … rain to concede.
At times the day looks split in two, as if nature cannot decide
and I could choose neither. … For me, there lies beauty in either side.

To the west of the valley.

To the east of the valley.

I do think the Highland climate tries to respect the summer's turn.
Oft rain is brief; and when clouds break the sun is hot enough to burn.
Alas its geology strikes and the seasonal norm rescinds,
with the formation of heavy rainclouds and whipping-up of winds.
I for one can forgive the weather's ever changing to's and fro's,
for by doing such it has crafted us a land rich in rainbows.

A land of rainbows.

To feel too fast again, time to take to bed for another night—
and expected to go with the switch … my last vestiges of sight.
Yet when accustomed come, my eyes look upward to a starlit scene.
By one who frequents suburbs is such saturation seldom seen.
As their numbers rise 'yond counting I shall a while this vigil keep.
Though sleepy, till I have feasted 'pon this grand reveal I cannot sleep.

A new morn brings forth to the breadth of this valley a haunting shroud,
which heavy hangs and muffles all sounds amidst the ground-hugging cloud.
Yet even as outside I step, a light air is driving it east
and in but minutes more the land around is from its veil released.
I turned perchance to see wide wings flap close to the grass 'pon the brae.
I know not what it was, though am glad from me … 'twas flying away.

A misty morning across the valley.

On the far side of Newtonmore, neath a sky of low cloud in grey,
to the Highland Folk Museum for a fine day I make my way.
The open-air eclectic mix of dwellings from this nation's past
shows us clearly how they lived then is quite an odd and stark contrast.
All looks small and very basic – even those nearer present day.
I would not be best pleased if modern trappings were taken away.

Part of the folk museum viewed from the café.

A highland cottage from the 1800s, originally located at Grantown-on-Spey.

Slightly peculiar and a tad invasive, it feels to me,
that wandering round a place which someone once called home I should be.
Yet what captivation is found and imaginings there evoked
as are these buildings from history's all-consuming swathe uncloaked!
Well done, Dr Grant, for your shrewd foresight and tireless endeavour.
Without your sense to save them, these gems would have been lost forever.

A tailor's shop, built by a father for his tailor son, returned wounded from World War 1.

A shepherd's bothy (made from railway sleepers), originally located near Dalwhinnie.

Through the woods and farther back still to the eighteenth-century site.
A small reconstructed settlement which will shed a little light
as to how people then coexisted as a community;
to see for yourself, it really is a good opportunity.
Players in period dress inform and help bring the scene to life.
A fascinating place to roam at leisure for me and my wife.

Part of the settlement, with one of the players in his blue hat.

A lack of wildlife, though a great let-down, alas is nothing new.
Away they shall vanish with the subtlest sight, sound or smell of you.
Though close by and of us aware, the chances of spotting them near…
well, let's just say you have as much hope of seeing Nessie, I fear.
But that makes the moment all the sweeter, with excitement increased.
A tale to regale o'er a dram, when you spot an elusive beast.

A random glance can have as much chance, so
keep you must those eyes peeled,
like when out today driving I spied four foals grazing in a field.
Then some while later, with a dash, devoid the faintest screech or squawk,
from a branch, in an instant on to flight, emerged a stealthy hawk.
This is the nature of the natural world, so easily missed.
A lucky spot – right time, right place – 'tween
trees, long grass or through Scotch mist.

Sadly, 'tis oft those ill-fated are the only wildlife to see,
that lingered too long or chose the wrong moment from the woods to flee.
For the roadsides are littered with a cast of unfortunate beast,
which from the rigours of their Highland survival are now released.
Though vehicles may damage sustain, they will pay the higher price.
To see such a devastating clash of worlds is not very nice.

Returning to the cottage, we pull in at the Caoldair craft shop.
Whenever around these parts, 'tis a place where often we will stop.
As long as there be cafés and tea rooms we shall wander content,
for after walking is to have hot meals and drinks money well spent.
Now energy by soup recouped, we cover the short journey back
to settle in and watch the dusk, down this old familiar track.

Next morn, to Newtonmore for fresh groceries and a Sunday Post,
then intent on a short amble, the length of the main street at most.
Yet across from the civic hall a sign on the wall reads 'Glen Road',
so down we turn and follow, past the church and many an abode.
'Fore we know we are out in the sticks, on a path towards the heights.
What a place to have on your doorstep, with such visual delights!

Unlike in autumn's onset, whereupon the fern shall the glen gild,
onward by perennial purple heather are the hillsides filled.
The younger sprig outdoes the older – fresher, with colour bolder.
This, plus varied thickness, lends subtle changes to the beholder.
Together with shifting light, their blankets 'pon the landscapes drape.
Magnificent in their multitude … hues of lilac, mauve and grape.

Beyond the far end of Glen Road.

Younger sprigs much brighter than the surrounding older ones.

Should the crashing might of a waterfall be your feature of choice,
to have other sounds about you muted by its thunderous voice,
to witness untamed torrents their part play to erode and reshape,
as on to the awaiting and much calmer river to escape.
Thus, with its high-sided steep valleys and an abundance of rain,
plus millennia of carving, plentiful here they shall remain.

Pattack Falls (A86 between Newtonmore and Spean Bridge) from observation deck.

Pattack Falls further downstream from the gorge.

A strange-looking 'seat' on the way to the Hermitage, Dunkeld.

This carved, contoured cone, a surprisingly restful posture provides,
so lie back and look up to where the stately Douglas fir presides.
For what better a way to study structures for their height renowned!
Novel indeed and very effective, when so close to the ground.
Of course I, once outstretched and still, could easily have taken root,
but upright I shall drag myself to see more sights of great repute.

Trees tower above you – gaze up through the branches without straining your neck.

The Black Linn Falls, near Dunkeld, from small stone bridge.

Black Linn Falls, Dunkeld, are of a particular ferocity.
Huge volumes of water crash down with great might and velocity.
Ossian's Hall: an interesting find which adds a certain mystique.
'Tis a charm to enter and pass through something so old and unique.
Though safe, the viewing balcony puts one uncomfortably close,
and displays, for all to see, a force impossible to oppose.

Ossian's Hall entrance.

Ossian's Hall viewing balcony, with stone bridge beyond.

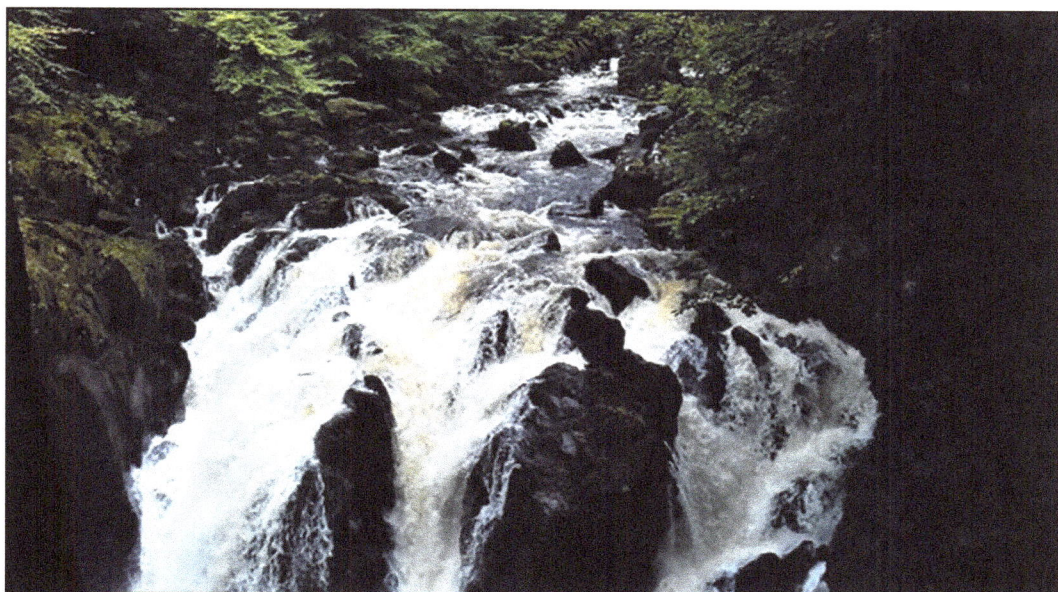

Black Linn Falls as viewed from Ossian's Hall.

Up the path from the hall the money tree is a quirky surprise.
This cut-up trunk, more copper than coppice, by the riverside lies.
Is good luck 'pon the visitor bestowed should a coin they imbed,
or is it just done as a copycat inclination instead?
So oft for no real reason the action of one others inspires.
The only good fortune it may bring: to a poor man with pliers.

Part of the money tree on the path alongside the falls.

Some yards further on by the tumbling River Braan the hermit's cave,
'tween huge boulders built o'er 200 years ago, stands grey and grave.
A stone corbelled roof sits atop walls of quite substantial thickness.
'Twould instil upon leaving not the merest hint of homesickness,
for 'tis austere in the extreme with just holes for windows and door;
no finer trappings therein – one bare rocky room and earthy floor.

The Hermitage, with daylight showing inside from one of the windows.

Moving on, follow the path, then sign a mile or so upriver
and to the Rumbling Bridge's smaller falls the track shall deliver.
A bridge 'pon a bridge the deep gorge to straddle, its sides too obscured.
Strain round the rocks for a better look – make sure you be well insured.
The drop down below, narrow and dark, is, to say the least, severe.
Not a place to lose one's footing – slippy-stoned, its sides gouged and sheer.

Rumbling Bridge Falls.

Rumbling Bridge Falls dropping down to pass under the small stone bridge.

To the largest town in the Highlands, Fort William, for a mosey,
where I shall don whenever here my spectacles tinted rosy.
For so many years ago a courting couple came by to stay
whilst on a coach trip, and the first time together on holiday.
From their hotel the street, not then pedestrianised, hummed with cars;
yet I cared not, for aloft with my love I was drifting through stars.

Fort William's pedestrianised street. The hotel has the flags on the wall.

Fort William looking towards the mountain range.

Though more amenities than any other town around may boast,
all these years on I am not sure which of us has changed the most.
Now long away are some shops in which browsing I used to enjoy,
and thus to find them gone does my sense to keep such untouched annoy.
To find things quaint, of older days … I like them to stay as they are.
To accept their closure – let them go – I do find rather bizarre.

I endorse not generic towns and would rather they stayed unique.
'Tis a faithful blend of modernity and heritage I seek.
'Tis nice to return and see familiar things, plus that newly found—
the bronze Model T Ford sculpture, with its true story to astound.
So we browse and buy the odd bits and bobs then join the traffic's flow
and once more leave this town I saw first over thirty years ago.

The bronze Model T Ford sculpture (not usually with fencing around).

With or without a car, Ben Nevis I have ne'er yet ascended.
I dare to think I may someday, 'fore my chance to try is ended.
With the tallest Munro and the lovely Loch Linnhe to attract,
for my liking, Fort William will always be by visitors packed.
But to the weary backpacker it must be a welcoming site—
to get dry indoors from the rain, which can be a long way from light.

The Jacobite (or Hogwarts Express) waiting to leave Fort William Station for Mallaig.

Awaiting the whistle and green flag waved, a brooding steam train stands,
soon to depart 'pon an adventure which praising plaudits demands.
One of the most scenic railway routes in the world ... thought by many.
Twice a passenger, words of disagreement I have not any.
First class if you can, and for the best views on the left be seated,
and to the most wondrous, stirring odyssey you will be treated.

By the side of the road looking north up Loch Linnhe.

By the side of the road looking south down Loch Linnhe.

Ben Nevis stands over 4,000 feet and for miles can be seen.
It may be walked via a path or climbed if you are really keen.
Easy to ascend, close to the town, many will try and be thrilled;
though show it respect – this is a mountain where people have been killed.
The Highlands are a playground, where the
outdoors types can have much fun,
yet they may soon find themselves by the weather and terrain outdone.

Ben Nevis, seen from the Caledonian Canal.

33

To Fort William's west, Neptune's Staircase marks the start for a good walk,
where you may cover a decent distance and still have breath to talk.
O'er seventy miles along towpath and forest tracks if you choose;
though if you should, take a tent, provisions and sturdy boots or shoes.
A couple of hours will suffice for me along the Great Glen.
Enjoy it nicely level and spot the odd critter now and then.

The line of canals, locks and lochs, the faultline; follows north-east-bound.
Two centuries on, now for leisurely pursuits its function found,
though 'twas conceived to help poor crofters by the clearances stricken.
A time when the landowners' greed could only offend and sicken,
when families were displaced from home to make way for flocks of sheep.
Lairds would destroy communities with ne'er a moment's loss of sleep.

Commencing a walk alongside the locks at Neptune's Staircase.

Though 'tis a cruel thought I harbour, which I have pondered oft before,
that the action of those landlords helped preserve this land I adore.
For around a century tenants their settlements vacated.
Had they not … by now, how many more towns may have been created?
I take no pleasure that such sparsity came at so high a cost;
yet had it ne'er happened, how much might be neath development lost?

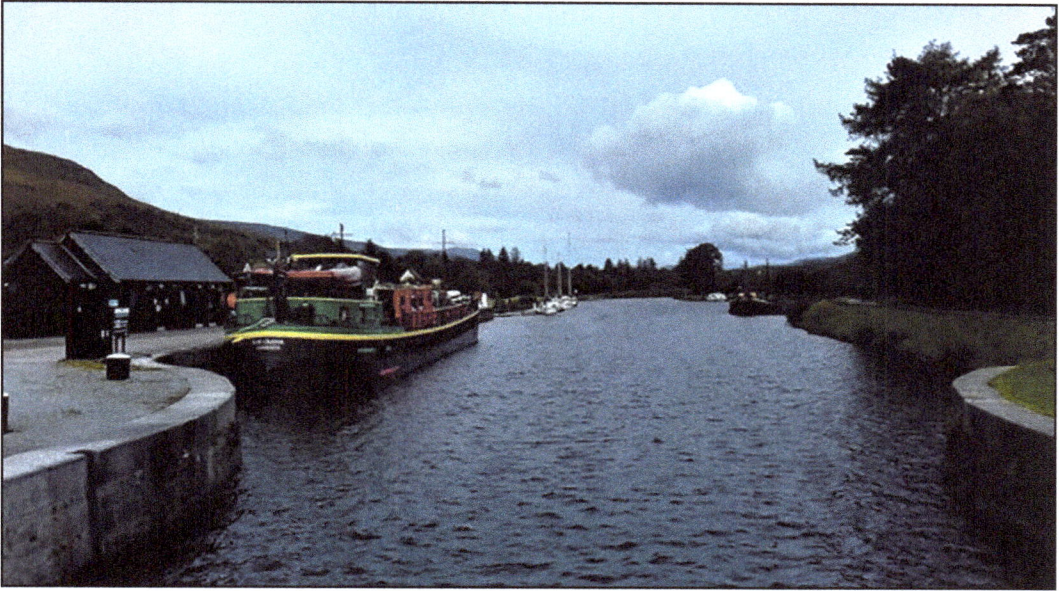

On the last lock before heading on towards Inverness.

Ten miles north is the obligatory stop-off at Spean Bridge Mill—
a centre we shall visit when we have a little while to kill.
All the usual tourist knick-knacks and bric-a-brac 'pon display;
one may look around, then have some lunch 'fore one carries on one's way.
All is there to care for my holiday wardrobe's every need
and adorn my middle-aged frame with Pringle, Field and Harris tweed.

Spean Bridge Mill.

35

Out the cottage and along the lane for a more testing ramble;
'tis thus on this occasion past bridge and cairn, then 'yond to scramble.
As here is not the old well-trodden routine 'pon which I enter,
for this time I shall reach the rock then turn slightly south of centre
'long a track ne'er 'fore by me traversed, which puts me high 'pon a peak,
as 'tis the elevated perspective of this land which I seek.

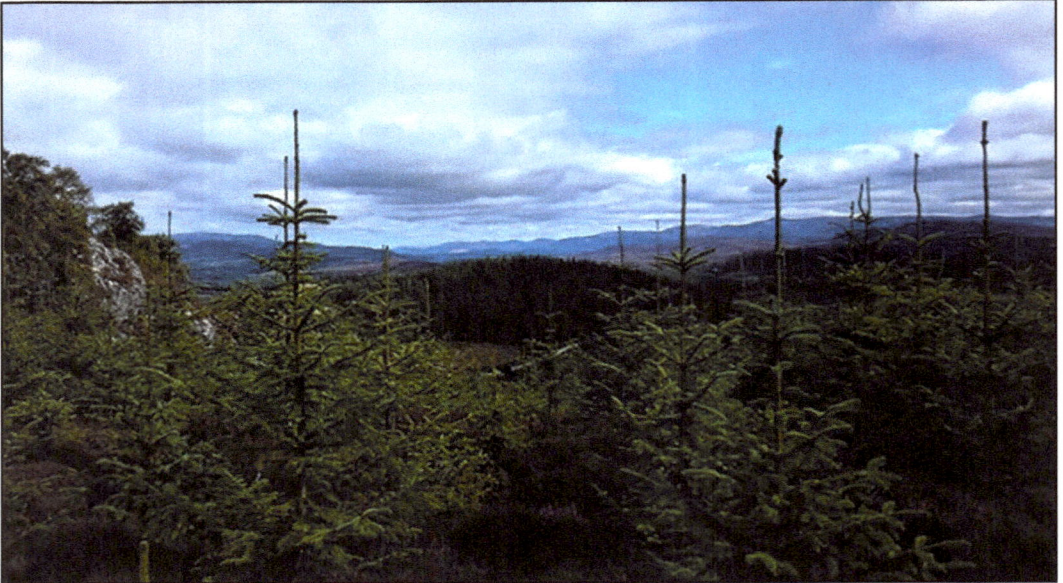

On the path approaching the viewing point, the sprawling peaks begin to appear.

Upon the viewing point, looking south-east.

With lungs nigh wrenched from ribs and strained
thighs which louder than banshees scream,
I am presented with a resplendent and much repeated theme,
for around, plus many onward unto all points of my facing,
the sight of mountains like Titans gathered are my eyes embracing.
From such marvel and tiredness equally dispensed I scan a-gasp,
as I my hands together in near religious reverence clasp.

Straight ahead, facing north.

For whom upon here could stand and not envy the birds' lofty view?
Man's inclusions are paltry by this vast comparison, 'tis true,
and looks with ease might be swallowed up should such whimsy nature take.
'Twould need a force of biblical degree to their foundations shake.
Surrounded by these ancient, majestic slabs, this frail human speck,
brief in its being, whilst these millennia more the land bedeck.

There I gaze … as my grievances of the world fade to the distance.
Who, to this spiritual replenishing could show resistance?
A bracing breeze about me swirls, like lost, wandering souls of old –
the fallen from conflicts in bloodied glens, their stories never told.
Static may be my body, but the mind like an eagle shall soar…
to ponder things then and see the now, so high from the valley floor.

Looking across the valley eastward.

Of course my stomach, as always, to stay quiet is refusing.
It cares not for nice views, such ambiance … higher, thoughtful musing.
So 'pon the bench provided I shall sit me down and have my lunch,
and oh, what a place, upon a ham sandwich and Scotch egg to munch!
Though an uplifting elixir, worth the energy expending,
now 'tis time to away, and much less taxing is the descending.

Looking across the valley westward.

With telltale signs that autumn approaches and soon shall take its hold,
quick to turn be the copious fern – green to yellow, bronze and gold.
Most of the deciduous trees are standing fast, save one or two,
which, under way, appear resigned to consider their summer through.
Though the equinox is a fortnight yet nature keeps no diary.
Plants can but sense the change and prepare for the seasons' expiry.

The fern feel autumn's early touch.

I find it quite snug and soothing to awake to the sound of rain,
as 'cross roof-tile slate it tap-dances and patters 'pon windowpane.
When neath the duvet I may remain in no mad rush to arise,
I should gladly lie and listen to it cascade down from the skies
and resent not its arrival, whilst I idle on warm and dry;
for this land would be less lush if the clime did such downfalls deny.

Around a ten-mile drive to Kingussie and eager to be fed,
where Café Aroma's breakfast sets me up for the day ahead.
Then out and right at the lights 'long Ardbroilach Road to head on up.
'Tis 'pon such inclines I am inclined to feel no more the young pup,
for thighs shall burn as hip bones groan and gravity's pull will berate
as past nice houses I go on till I reach the Pitmain Estate.

Looking towards Ardbroilach Road, which gets steeper as it goes.

A pleasant walk now levelled out near the river, rocky and low.
Rusty-grey bark on towering trunks, straight and narrow, row 'pon row.
'Long the banks silver birch and other species cluster and compete,
as within the branches I see red squirrels scamper and retreat.
The path cuts in two the golf course, where there are wayward balls to dodge,
then carries on a decent way to the private well-gated lodge.

Towering trunks along the roadside.

The view over the far side of the river (with the moon still slightly visible).

'Pon a rougher track follow the water to the start of the moor,
which lies beyond the fence – a vast expanse, full of life, I am sure.
Yet for me it harbours little allure, other than its extent.
Within its breathtaking bleakness it lacks that which leaves me content.
I need trees to pervade the world around me … no genus favoured.
Countryside is with them complete and are walks amongst them savoured.

The start of the moor.

How much nicer a view with trees.

'Tis time to head back, so downhill all the way on to the main street,
with sweat 'pon my brow, jacket removed and loudly complaining feet.
For the day, not as forecast, has been unexpectedly sunny,
which, when both prepared for rain, is a bit of a pain … not funny.
Now we are set to visit the garrison – 'tis not very far;
but after that trudge my bones cannot budge, so we shall go by car.

Stopped at the railway crossing en route to the old garrison.

Sat sternly 'pon a natural strategic vantage – a good spot
to dissuade and quell a dangerous breed: the rebellious Scot.
Built in response to one uprising though would not survive the next,
Ruthven Barracks could not withstand such big numbers, suitably vexed.
Lastly it fell to the beleaguered and dispersing Jacobite,
who left it how it still looks today, after setting it alight.

Ruthven Barracks.

An abundance of ruins stands testimony to Scotland's past.
Once-sturdy strongholds, overwhelmed by force or razed by cannon blast.
Long-lost leaders called them home and men within their walls would rally
and watch enemies approach along the loch, moorland or valley.
Now reduced to more resemble a folly in the weather's grip,
which o'er the generations will continue to wear down and chip.

The threat of a downpour loiters – a reminder that summer wanes
and that we should make the most of the sun before the autumn gains.
Now back at the house, I rest; then with a crumb of vigour restored,
out 'long the lane I go neath clouds with water collected and stored,
ready 'twould look to strike with a deluge and saturate the land.
And I hope if it does, 'tis something my waterproofs can withstand.

Heading up the lane on my late-afternoon walk ... towards a forbidding sky.

Yet amazingly I complete my excursion foot-worn but dry,
for howe'er much water-laden clouds are, it remains in the sky.
I think therefore this night's slumber shall have a rainy serenade.
Better then, I believe, than on till the following day delayed.
Though intent perhaps to relent the heavens look as shafts break through,
who up here can know, for the climate will do what it chooses to?

'Tis a tease indeed this impish Highland weather, faux and fickle.
Sometimes the skies look fit to burst, yet yield no more than a trickle;
others begin neath blue sky and sun then end in an Arctic squall.
A taste of each season – 'tis common in one day to have them all.
'Tis hard to know, come each dawn, whether you shall be caressed or caught.
There be times where light and colours look
more from an artist's brush brought.

As if this place does not already seem to me touched divinely,
rays splay through parting clouds to strike the treeline and fields benignly.
Even a farmer's gate a way to heaven may be mistaken.
Though flight of fancy, here from suchlike 'tis hard to awaken.
Thus I continue on whilst breathing deep the fresh unsullied air,
back for an evening of music, malt and wife's sweet company there.

As the clouds start to disperse beams of light shine through.

She, like me, the Highlands loves and could readily move here to stay.
How then would I feel indeed in paradise each entrancing day?
For though I adore this glorious land and there may walk alone,
I do so knowing that she is nearby, for she my heart does own.
How hollow and bereft of lasting bliss would my enjoyment be
if my darling Gillian was not here to share it all with me!

Making my way back, the clouds continue to clear without a drop of rain falling.

A quiet morning.

All is still in the valley.

A nice quiet start to the morn, with coffee, toast and marmalade,
then off to Pitlochry in the old jalopy the way is made.
For my wife, from the daily miles of walking, more retail respite.
All day she could flit in and out of each outlet in sheer delight.
Even if not one purchase made, 'twould not downturn her smiling face.
Blithely all her time she could spend, embroiled in the thrill of the chase.

*Atholl Road, Pitlochry. Can you see the false window painted
to look like a lady sat by her open curtains?*

Thus, having been much merchandise perusing – and more cash to part—
to locate somewhere to get some lunch we thought we should make a start.
So, as you do, we wandered down to the hydroelectric dam.
For to make such a choice you might think I have snuck a sneaky dram.
But the visitors'-centre café is not a bad place to eat.
If you like impressive engineering, the view is hard to beat.

The hydroelectric dam visitors' centre.

Hydroelectric dam from the visitors'-centre balcony.

Alas, the pandemic another annual spectacle claims,
for around this date we should enjoy the Pitlochry Highland Games.
To see the bands parade the street with their resounding pipes and drums,
'tis hard to impassive remain and soon all who watches succumbs.
Colourful tartans, rousing music ancestral feelings revive,
and so alongside we follow till 'pon the playing fields arrive.

The gathering is under way, and what an event to witness!
Head to head they compete, to be the victor in strength and fitness.
A most entertaining day, so much to see, nice food to nibble;
and though the day for two may be quite pricey, I would not quibble,
for a truly Highland experience is had come sun or rain
and memories which you take away you shall forever retain.

Thus the recollections of last year will have to for now suffice,
though should the chance permit to attend again I would ne'er think twice.
With calories yet to expend, whilst legs on walking still willing
I drive back north, park up and seek the place I find most fulfilling.
From the layby a tricky trek 'long the road of walkway wanting;
and when log-laden lorries pass, the task may be somewhat daunting.

My favoured stroll to Ardverikie House from the gatehouse embarks,
with a 'what's to come' flavour as to a more flamboyant past harks;
for designed to impress, grey-stoned and gorgeous by the bridge it stands.
Its turret and Gothic lines the notice of all who pass commands.
Well I recall the first time I took this way, 'gainst right-angled rain
and with wind-flung frame in weather which seemed to my presence disdain.

The gatehouse and bridge.

On 'tween two pointy pillars and o'er a small criss-cross metal bridge,
'long the grey tarmac track, thankfully plagued not by the dreaded midge;
on forth we go past wide-spreading sands to follow Loch Laggan's line,
vigilant as we pass tall evergreen and ever sprawling pine;
for in there, somewhere, twice seen by me before, red squirrels scurry.
Though a keen eye keep, for fleet of fur they be … gone in a flurry.

Left of the loch and flanked by tree lines, the driveway extends ahead,
where shall be taken many steps and these poor boots will lose more tread.
'Twill be worth the weary wandering for I know what there awaits:
the stone-and-mortar marvel which to a glamorous world relates.
So I soldier on, blisters bear and try to take it in my stride,
though the giddy gushing for where I am is difficult to hide.

Looking from the path towards the beach.

To spend time in my presence 'bout these parts, 'tis fairly plain to see,
not the best of bedfellows be our encroachment 'pon land and me.
Yet one intrusion I must applaud: the saviour of foot and tyre.
A smoothly paved way tarmac creates – keeps you from the muddy mire.
Not mainly one to be pleased with soil being lost neath things man-made,
with such treacherous topography … a vital part it has played.

On the lookout for the elusive red squirrel.

Just off the road the side slopes steeply down to the loch banks.

'Yond narrow grass verges with edges by countless pine needles strewn,
lies terrain to keep me on the straight and narrow this afternoon.
For one side drops away to the rocky loch banks beyond the trees;
the other rises into woodland which no one could pass with ease,
as mossy lumps and bumps with scattered debris and toppled tinder—
any attempt to navigate through their chance would surely hinder.

To the left the side is rocky, mossy and almost impassable.

The long road up to the big house.

Then soon after the appearance of iron railings 'pon the right,
once again am I captivated by the much awaited sight.
For as opens up the vista, the big house comes into my view
and I could swear by my reaction I am finding it anew.
As if first time seen, or some fine features having ne'er 'fore noted
and that more time 'pon its scrutiny should be keenly devoted.

Ardverike House.

Of grey stone too which shines bright in sunlight or stands sullen in rain.
Moods by weather determined, yet its fairy-tale looks shall remain.
This striking Victorian edifice mimics an older style;
and every time I face it, I have to stand in awe a while.
With towers and turrets 'pon each vantage neath pointed slated cone.
Busy of build, a splendid assault to my eyes I ne'er bemoan.

Alas, the access to wander within its walls I ne'er have had.
Given the nod to delve 'yond each doorway, I should gratefully gad.
What dazzling discoveries of period features there abound?
The craftsman's skill and attention to detail shall always astound.
Yet unless attending a function or wedding I might ne'er know.
At least, for me, its outside splendour always puts on a good show.

View from the back of the walled garden.

And all the while, as I enjoy and savour this panorama,
are scenes recalled, like warming memories, of a much loved drama.
In my mind's eye the characters I see clearly 'fore me like ghosts,
as to Glenbogle I walk to share a dram with my phantom hosts.
When here I cannot help but from real life to this fantasy drift,
as it has for years been a dream to which I would happily shift.

Back to reality … now with sandwiches had I must away
and harbour the slightest envy for those who dwell here day 'pon day.
I trust they reflect 'pon their good fortune, ne'er take it for granted,
for they live in a surrounding I see as truly enchanted.
No midge bite nor wintry wind would sentiments for here rescind,
for of this journey is my liking for the region underpinned.

To the Victorians I give thanks, for they fashioned the estates,
brought in new flora and fauna, grand expressions built 'yond their gates.
Though done for their own approval and the impressing of their peers,
they left a legacy in which I have revelled for years and years.
For was their proclaiming of nature and opulence in design
a template which the character of the whole Highlands would define.

Who cannot be impressed by the artistry of Victorian design? It transcends function.

Whilst there we chanced 'pon the owner's daughter and husband out walking.
We exchanged passing greetings then spent a few minutes more talking.
Though by comparison seemed their dogs had better breeding than me,
the couple's brief company was wholly pleasant in which to be.
Then up pulled a van – the driver with the lady needed to chat—
so with a goodbye on we headed and that was the end of that.

Another misty morn, which through the rising sun's rays slowly reach,
as west I go, Morar-bound then off left for Camusdarach Beach.
Walk o'er the small wooden bridge and the narrow path forward proceed.
That which lies forth, might it underwhelm or expectations exceed?
As sandier grows the way, a wall of grassy dunes left appear
and my excitement builds as sounds, round the corner, are drawing near.

Follow the path ... what shall be revealed?

The path opens up into sand dunes.

Rounding the corner, the beach comes into view.

Into the sea runs the river as I watch the bay open out,
with a white sand which can almost dazzle and leaves me in no doubt
that a special coastline indeed this is when the clear sky beams blue,
whilst on the hazy horizon the islands cluster – what a view!
A seashore by which to while as many hours as you may care
and plunge your feet in the skin-quivering cold briny if you dare.

The beach stretches out with Eigg and Rum on the horizon.

On top of the grass-covered rocky coastline looking north (Skye on the left horizon).

To pass from beach to cove or o'er grassy tops, the routes may vary;
but should you choose a path through the dense, matted bushes, be wary.
There shall you be enveloped by an intrusive thicket of thorn,
where those of wide girth or reckless pace may
have skin scratched … clothing torn.
Still, to walk 'long the edge of lapping tides or sit 'pon rocky tops,
or watch life teeming in pools … 'tis worth making this one of your stops.

One of the small coves with broad swathes of thorny bushes on the hillside onwards.

Mallaig main street.

Once again the call of lunch cannot be ignored, so sand in tread,
back in the car, onward three miles up the road to Mallaig I head.
An energetic port which survives on tourism and fishing.
With its large ferry a means if to go by sea you are wishing
to visit the Isle of Skye, with amazing vistas end to end.
Not for me to be on water – 'tis not my chosen way to wend.

Downhill towards the harbour.

Another day-out done, back to Laggan 'long sunny roads to make.
Later 'pon my regular constitutional I undertake,
for the exercise mainly, though of the views I shall not tire.
I should gladly the route thus repeat, if walked but hours prior.
Who could not wish to holiday here, so beautiful and remote?
To 'pon this way again decide will always get my hearty vote.

The rip-roaring RAF is a singular oddness of mine.
One might think I would object most strongly to their merest outline.
'Twould appear such juxtaposition does not my karma impede,
for breathtaking indeed their incursion I find – the noise and speed.
Though I baffle myself at times, the novelty would soon wear thin,
I am sure, if too oft assaulted the skies their deafening din.

Across the valley from the narrow road ... with cartoon clouds.

Remaining local for this morning's saunter and the sun does bask.
A short jaunt o'er the way to Laggan is all of the car I ask.
Parked near the village hall, we head off 'cross the cattle grid and on.
'Tis quite satisfying when here, how soon all thoughts of time are gone.
The road bends to follow the Spey past Coul Farm, its name etched in stone;
on to the dam, a slight blot, though its relevance one must condone.

The view to the left whilst walking away from Laggan.

Approaching the small dam.

Onward some yards more and the stony path breaks off to the first gate,
which marks the start of the track through the mountains and I cannot wait.
Though in a harsh storm it may not be the place you might wish to be,
with its feral beauty … gift of solitude, it is dear to me.
Dumbstruck that another hot day should be down upon us bearing,
the walking is perhaps more laboured with exertions now sparing.

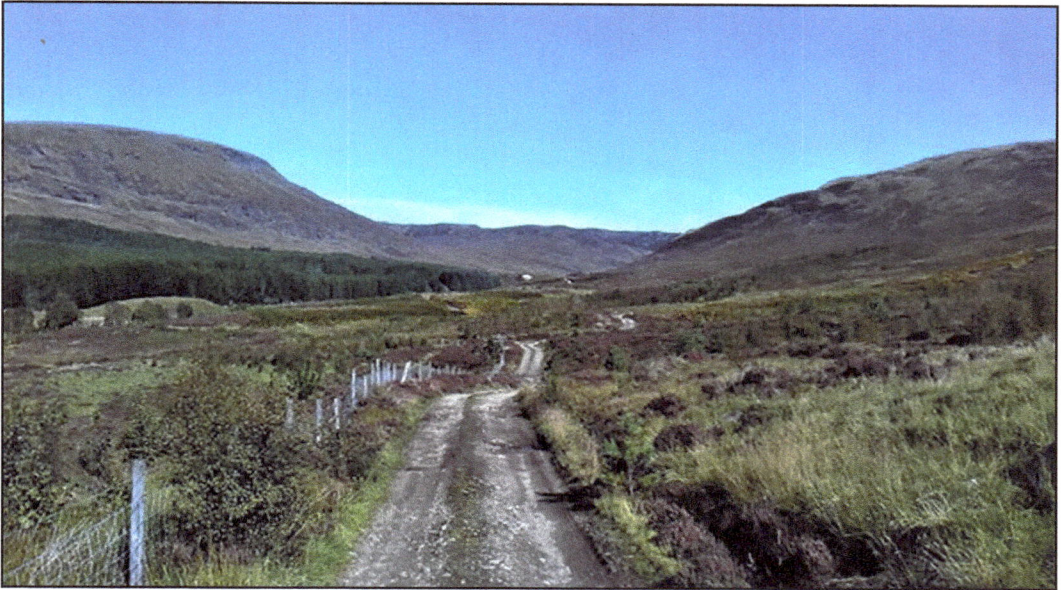

The track leading into the mountain pass.

A lot can happen in little time … yet up here the pace seems slow.
Like the rocks' erosion or sweeping forests which steadily grow.
Perhaps with great bias I feel here a peace I can rarely find,
as if only this wilderness may bring such unity of mind.
Could it be to feel so small 'gainst nature's scale one's spectres demeans?
A cleansing therapy, to walk amongst and wallow in such scenes.

As the path continues we draw closer to the woodland.

The path continues into the glen as lower down the rocky river flows.

The approaching evergreens look inviting, if only for shade,
let alone for what animals our prying eyes there evade.
Greatly valued would be just the merest morsel of a sighting.
To catch them a riverside drink snatching would be most exciting.
But for flagging endurance I should gladly continue all day;
thus, with dogs a-barking, too soon back to the car we are away.

The winding water on its way to join the Spey. How often do deer nip out for a drink?

'Tis so loud, the call of Caledonia … I can ne'er resist.
Its grandest fabric radiates to my core and will there persist.
Hence this tonic, this drug, fore'er shall be found for me alluring
and nothing of it I encounter may make it less enduring
within my restless desire to pray one day up here remain.
Its moody majesty needs me not to exaggerate nor feign.

Though folks through maps and glossy brochures
may choose trips – fine if they do,
for tourist traps are worth the visit – will not disappoint 'tis true.
But the Highlands have such a plethora of natural beauty,
to off and gallivant for myself I consider my duty.
With care, to commit to memory or trap 'yond camera lens;
for the prepared intrepid wanderer there is a glut of glens.

And what a change in the weather's direction this new morning takes!
As limbs be tired we wait to see if it for the better breaks.
A good chance to top up supplies and have a more inactive day,
since it appears this inclement turn for a while is here to stay.
So on with the kettle, then get those stacked-up logs lit and roaring;
then out to the bridge I walk… Naught shall stop me this land adoring.

Approaching the cottage through the drizzle.

63

Thus autumn arrives damp and dreich with hills in a watery haze,
and as the rain soaks through my pants I appreciate drier days.
A lack of leggings allows the blustering wind to chill the skin.
Howe'er, I know the house is close and I will soon be back within.
The open fire awaits my return with embers of orange glow,
where I shall sit and warm my bones from heated head to toasty toe.

'Tis simple fact one bad-weather day does not a holiday spoil.
Not up here, where it can rain non-stop for days and all your plans foil.
Some sad souls have so endured and vowed never to this way return,
and found its swift changeability a bitter lesson to learn.
'Tis a risk I shall always be happy to take … for even now
the sky clears as sets the sun, which lights the land whilst it takes its bow.

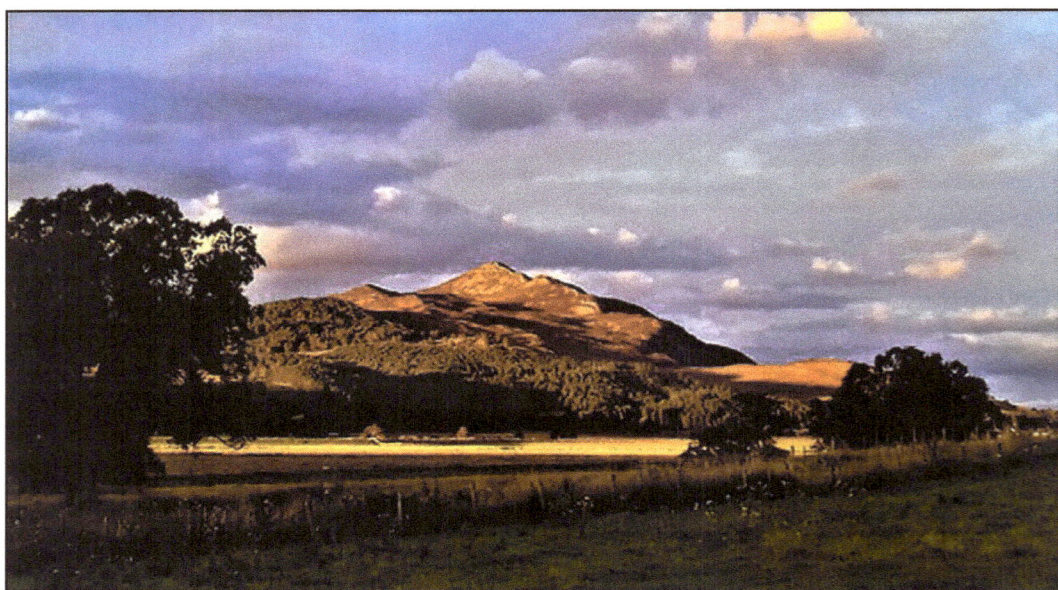

A lovely sunset after a miserable day.

Farther a travel today as to Fort Augustus out I set,
for there be a famous landmark 'pon which we have not looked as yet.
As distractions en route our good speed slows, I pull in to see
the Commando Memorial … to men who fought to keep us free.
A reminder of how the surrounding terrain helped brave men train
for the endurances of warfare … to sharpen body and brain.

The Commando Memorial by the A82 north of Spean Bridge.

Not too far on, aside Loch Lochy, the road skims along its banks.
How could I not halt, admire the peaks which 'pon the other side flanks!
Though to falter, our destination we shall reach soon enough;
but such views must be seen 'fore the weather draws in too wet and rough.
Conditions as thus should ne'er be thought lasting and lightly taken,
for in time's briefest passage are chances to see clear forsaken.

By the road up to Fort Augustus passing Loch Lochy and mountains beyond.

In due course we park up in the Fort Augustus pay and display
and for an hour or two for a nosy around we shall stay.
Among gongoozlers to watch some boats the
locks descend, Loch Ness-bound.
Nice craft … though both feet I would sooner keep firmly upon the ground.
One final obstacle to negotiate 'fore their way is clear.
The time now approaches as onlookers and vessels gather near.

Fort Augustus.

Further up the locks, looking towards Loch Ness.

So with audible alarm and flashing lights the barriers drop
and from either direction the road traffic is brought to a stop,
whilst in single file the skippers, slow ahead through the channel chug,
whence to its resting position the swing bridge returns nice and snug.
Free now their unhurried cruise to pursue along the loch north-east,
as motor vehicles impatient from their long wait are released.

Boats pass through the open swing bridge.

When Highland-bound one has to visit this loch of monstrous romance.
Does Nessie lurk within the depths out 'yond in such a great expanse?
Near twenty-three miles long, o'er seven hundred feet deep … space to hide;
with caves, nooks and crannies where a creature might furtively reside.
'Tis a fanciful notion which I hope is actually true;
yet I pray the mystery remains as thus for aeons anew.

Such a capacity of water I struggle to comprehend,
though its grandeur is immediately understood … to transcend
stories of some artful detection dodger lurking neath unseen.
For sheer imposing stature, as Loch Ness 'long mountains stretches 'tween,
this image which lies 'fore me does thrill and chill in equal measure,
yet will be one nonetheless which I shall take with me and treasure.

Loch Ness. No, you have not spotted the monster in the bottom right. It's a duck.

After a meander and casual gander 'tis time to go.
Come later on, I have my predictable lone walk … to and fro.
Though difficult with such views, sometimes it pays to lower the head.
Not only for animal waste should you be careful where you tread.
The loveliness of nature is not always found in grander scale –
too easily you might miss something worth seeing along the trail.

A brightly coloured fungus by the side of the road. I would not want to eat it.

And thus arrives with neither fanfare nor welcome the last full day,
whereupon, with morning stillness to savour, I walk 'long the way
to look back at the cottage and farm 'yond. Tomorrow I shall leave.
What I would give, like one condemned, to get a last-minute reprieve
and dally here evermore till with us all the rapture reckons?
Yet of course all good things must end, though one more excursion beckons.

The last full morning – walking back to the cottage after a short pre-breakfast stroll.

At the end of Loch Shiel, Glenfinnan is settled amongst the crags,
where through the arches stretches the estate, home for buzzards and stags.
In the main, most visitors the centre and monument frequent,
then a good spot find themselves … in hope of a train their time then spent.
I prefer to cross over and walk along the loch valley track,
or disappear 'yond Concrete Bobs creation with stick and backpack.

Along the main road to the lane by the river with care to take,
then neath the viaduct into the estate 'long the path we snake.
The most famous railway span in Scotland, after the Forth and Tay,
lest, of course, fans of a bespectacled young wizard should have their say,
whereupon with such ranking I am sure would as one disagree.
And why would I dispute their point? One of those fans may well be me!

Towards Loch Shiel from the road, with the Glenfinnan monument on the left.

'Twas once but two types of tourist by this curved bridge would assemble,
until more recently the line to Hogwarts it should resemble.
Now the steam-train buff and photo opportunist for space must vie
with would-be sorcerers to watch the Hogwarts Express chuffing by.
Named rather the Jacobite … Fort William to Mallaig twice a day.
A magical sight as it slowly makes o'er each striding archway.

Passing under the Glenfinnan Viaduct.

Once past a nestle of cottages people are left way behind
and 'tis the lack of human activity so calming I find.
To me, nature always seems in better balance and less restrained
when a goodly gap between it and humankind can be maintained.
I have nothing against my fellow Homo sapiens per se;
'tis just, I should much rather find myself from them farther away.

To a rather binding antisocial leaning I must admit;
hence to find any sense of well-being in hordes I am unfit.
'Tis not always the failings of others to cause me such alarm;
I am ill at ease regardless, though this land my issues disarm.
Its remoteness bestows 'pon me the solace I greatly require.
How could one not in such serenity more peaceably respire?

Heading into the estate with Glenfinnan Lodge in the distance.

Near the bothy, beside the river we eat sandwiches and rest,
and now whilst sat and cooling I feel more appropriately dressed.
'Tis a no-win situation choosing the best outdoor attire;
for once walking any distance, despite the weather I perspire.
Only when sedentary I appreciate the layers more.
I generally tend to overdress when I up here explore.

The bothy.

The track on from this blue-roofed shelter goes further into the glen,
though 'tis more of a struggle: steeper slopes and rocky now and then.
One perhaps for the tougher breed, though once conquered a treat awaits;
for far beyond Loch Arkaig sprawls … and in the valley dominates.
'Twould be nice to have the physical wherewithal for such a slog;
alas, I believe to attempt it would be a dead horse to flog.

Heading back out of the estate.

To visit or not – two things shall have people's opinion swaying.
The Scottish climate lends itself most aptly to the old saying:
'There is no such thing as bad weather, but only the wrong clothing.'
Ignore if you will, though your holiday you may end up loathing.
Howe'er the climate presents, do take waterproofs and something warm.
'Tween May and September beware should
those blood-sucking midges swarm.

A menace indeed is the marauding midge, feared in great numbers,
and once set 'pon your person 'tis fair to say your day encumbers,
for will be felt across the skin a bitch of an itch manyfold
as through hair, in ears, nostrils and eyes they bring misery untold.
'Tis no surprise, the collective noun for these wee brutes is a 'bite'.
To encounter them with no protection is far from a delight.

Though fret not, repellents are abundant, to be purchased with ease
and not everywhere Highland-bound is blighted by these flying fleas.
The heat or frost they dislike, and when winds rise up they are grounded.
Alas, during summer months you are more likely to be hounded.
So come prepared, lest you have the misfortune to meet them en masse
and you find for yourself how it feels when 'pon your flesh they trespass.

To me, holidays here can pick your pocket – prices may be steep –
yet then again I would suggest that, for I want the best … but cheap.
A seasonal place in fairness, thus for many a shorter year;
so they have to make the most while they can, hence they may be quite dear.
But, that said, for UK tourist hotspots 'tis really quite the norm
and even an old skinflint the likes of me will gladly conform.

Howe'er, views you seek out yourself are priceless in more ways than one
and plentiful in their finding … though oft' with rather little sun.
Revel in such rovings and what recollections you shall take home…
to be so pleased with yourself you exercised your right to roam.
Just one basic request: respect the Highlands and leave them as found.
Sully not – be it in the air, of waterways or 'pon the ground.

Heed thee well and a fabulous vacation by all shall be had.
If dramatic landscapes you cherish, to come here you will be glad.
Of people and a land reaching back through the farthest history;
Clans who protected and battled, bathed in blood, myth and mystery.
Yet a warmth of character and friendly reception you shall find.
True Highlanders will welcome all – are known to be helpful and kind.

For always when about these parts, be it central or western coast,
might I relax, as are my entrenched stresses mollified the most.
Dare I think we might buy a humble house 'fore too long or too late?
The wish may brim with hope, yet an influx my slim reserves await.
Oft with schemes and daydreams of a Highland life I have regaled her.
To not fulfil her long-held desire I will feel to have failed her.

My last night … and how the trick of time has cheated me in its speed!
A restless one, for thoughts of leaving have me most troubled indeed.
As unwelcomed as self-pity, pangs of melancholy descend,
yet to terms I must come that my holiday thus is at an end.
Here my slumbers were just for rest, as through the daytime were my dreams.
After tonight they must return to the confines of sleep regimes.

The road passing the cottage heading back to the military road – the way home.

The weeks passed unfairly fast and 'fore 'tis known we are soon away.
Not yet gone I pray for a speedy return and one day to stay.
The child within could sob once more as sadness looms that he must leave;
the notion to ne'er again frequent this land he could not perceive.
My being feels incomplete when my perceptions these landscapes lack.
Rest assured, 'pon the moment I am able, I shall haste me back.

www.ingramcontent.com/pod-product-compliance
Lightning Source LLC
Chambersburg PA
CBHW061419090426
42744CB00018B/2073

* 9 7 8 0 7 2 2 3 5 1 6 7 3 *